Full STEAM Ahead!
Technology Time

Technology
Then and Now

Cynthia O'Brien

CRABTREE
PUBLISHING COMPANY
WWW.CRABTREEBOOKS.COM

Title-Specific Learning Objectives:

Readers will:

- Understand that technology improves over time to make life easier, safer, and more fun.
- Identify some everyday technologies and ways that they have improved.
- Make connections between ideas in the text by comparing technologies in the past and present.

High-frequency words (grade one)	Academic vocabulary
a, and, are, had, has, have, is, it, make, the, was	equipment, instruments, materials, slate, technology

Before, During, and After Reading Prompts:

Activate Prior Knowledge and Make Predictions:

Have children read the title and look at the images on the cover and title page. Ask:

- What do you think this book will be about?
- What technologies do you see on the cover? How are they the same? How are they different? (Repeat for the image on the title page.)
- Can you think of another technology that has changed over time?

During Reading:

After reading any page that compares technology, ask children to look for connections in the text. For example, after reading pages 12 and 13, ask:

- What technology do you see on page 12? How do you know it has changed over time?
- What words tell you that the pictures on pages 12 and 13 are connected? (The first, Today, etc.)

After Reading:

Have children choose one example of a technology from the book and use a Venn diagram to compare and contrast the "past" and "present" versions.
They should pick out descriptive words from the text, and examine the pictures to come up with their own words, and insert them into the diagram.

Author: Cynthia O'Brien

Series Development: Reagan Miller

Editor: Janine Deschenes

Proofreader: Melissa Boyce

STEAM Notes for Educators: Reagan Miller and Janine Deschenes

Guided Reading Leveling: Publishing Solutions Group

Cover, Interior Design, and Prepress: Samara Parent

Photo research: Cynthia O'Brien and Samara Parent

Production coordinator: Katherine Berti

Photographs:
iStock: selimaksan: p. 5 (top); mediaphotos: p. 11; dpmike: p. 12
Shutterstock: A. Sontaya: p. 8; Ivan Kurmyshov: p. 9;
    Jerry Sharp: p. 19
Wikimedia: Adrian Pingstone: p. 18; Argonne National
    Laboratory: p. 20
All other photographs by Shutterstock

Library and Archives Canada Cataloguing in Publication

O'Brien, Cynthia (Cynthia J.), author.
       Technology then and now / Cynthia O'Brien.

(Full STEAM ahead!)
Includes index.
Issued in print and electronic formats.
ISBN 978-0-7787-6203-4 (hardcover).--
ISBN 978-0-7787-6240-9 (softcover).--ISBN 978-1-4271-2259-9 (HTML)

       1. Technological innovations--Juvenile literature.
2. Inventions--Juvenile literature. 3. Technology--History--Juvenile
literature. 4. Technology--Juvenile literature. I. Title.

T173.8.O27 2019   j609   C2018-906163-4
                                                    C2018-906164-2

Library of Congress Cataloging-in-Publication Data

Names: O'Brien, Cynthia, author.
Title: Technology then and now / Cynthia O'Brien.
Description: New York, New York : Crabtree Publishing Company, 2019.
   Series: Full STEAM ahead! | Includes index.
Identifiers: LCCN 2018056589 (print) | LCCN 2018059399 (ebook) |
   ISBN 9781427122599 (Electronic) |
   ISBN 9780778762034 (hardcover : alk. paper) |
   ISBN 9780778762409 (pbk. : alk. paper)
Subjects: LCSH: Technology--History--Juvenile literature. |
   Inventions--History--Juvenile literature.
Classification: LCC T48 (ebook) | LCC T48 .O273 2019 (print) |
   DDC 609--dc23
LC record available at https://lccn.loc.gov/2018056589

Printed in the U.S.A./042019/CG20190215

Table of Contents

Crabtree Publishing Company

www.crabtreebooks.com   1-800-387-7650

Copyright © **2019 CRABTREE PUBLISHING COMPANY**. All rights reserved. No part of this publication may be reproduced, stored in a retrieval system or be transmitted in any form or by any means, electronic, mechanical, photocopying, recording, or otherwise, without the prior written permission of Crabtree Publishing Company. In Canada: We acknowledge the financial support of the Government of Canada through the Book Publishing Industry Development Program (BPIDP) for our publishing activities.

Published in Canada	**Published in the United States**	**Published in the United Kingdom**	**Published in Australia**
Crabtree Publishing	Crabtree Publishing	Crabtree Publishing	Crabtree Publishing
616 Welland Ave.	PMB 59051	Maritime House	Unit 3 – 5 Currumbin Court
St. Catharines, Ontario	350 Fifth Avenue, 59th Floor	Basin Road North, Hove	Capalaba
L2M 5V6	New York, New York 10118	BN41 1WR	QLD 4157

Changing Technology

Technology is the tools that help us do work.

Some technologies make life safer.

Some technologies make life easier.

Some technologies make life more fun.

Over time, technology has changed. People have found new ways to make life easier, safer, and more fun.

The first televisions had small screens. Today, televisions have big screens! They are easier and more fun to watch.

Travel in the Sky

An airplane is a technology. It helps make **travel** easier. It helps us get from place to place very quickly.

The first airplane was small. It did not fly very quickly or very high in the sky. The first flight lasted about 12 seconds.

Today, airplanes travel very quickly! They fly high above the clouds. They can carry many people.

Cars Then and Now

A car is a technology that makes travel easier too. Do you travel in a car?

A car long ago had three wheels and no roof. It had a seat for two people.

Cars today are easier to travel in. They have roofs and four wheels.
They have seats for many people.

Changes at School

We use technologies at school to help make learning easier or more fun.

slate

wooden bench

Classrooms long ago were very different. Students sat together on long, wooden benches. They wrote with chalk on a **slate**.

In classrooms today, students sit at desks. They write with pencils on paper. They even use computers to make learning more fun!

computer

chair

desk

paper

pencil

What classroom technologies make your learning easier?

Cell Phones

A cell phone helps make it easier for people to talk to each other.

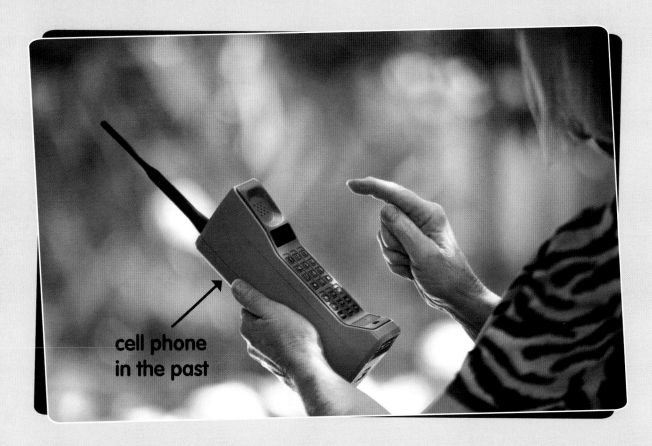

cell phone
in the past

The first cell phones were big and heavy. They were too big to put in your pocket! They did not have a camera or games to play.

cell phone
today

Today, cell phones are small. They are easy to take anywhere.
They are more fun to use too. They have cameras and games to play.

Playing Sports

People have always made technologies to make life more fun. Sports **equipment** makes life fun!

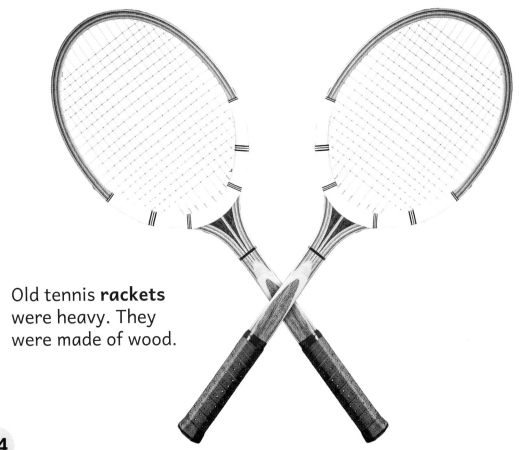

Old tennis **rackets** were heavy. They were made of wood.

Today, tennis rackets are made from a different **material**.
The new material makes the rackets very light.
This makes it easier to hit the tennis ball.

Making Music

Instruments are technologies that help people make music. They make life more fun!

animal skin

wood

Early drums were made from wood and animal skin. Some people still make music with drums like these.

Drums today are made of many materials, such as plastic. Different materials make different sounds.

drum machine

A drum **machine** can make the same sound as a drum!

Fighting Fire

A fire truck is a technology that makes life safer.

Long ago, fire trucks were pulled by horses or people. The trucks had buckets of water to help stop fires.

Today, fire trucks have **engines**. They can travel to fires quickly. They have long hoses and ladders. This helps firefighters stop fires more easily.

Computers

A computer is a technology that can make life easier, safer, and more fun!

The first computers were as big as a whole room!
They had many wires and buttons. They were hard to use.

laptop

Computers today are easier to use. They are smaller too.
Laptops are computers that you can carry everywhere.

Words to Know

engine [EN-juh n] noun Part of a machine that makes it work or move

equipment [ih-KWIP-muhnt] noun Things used for a certain purpose

instruments [IN-struh-muh nts] noun Tools that make musical sounds

machine [muh-SHEEN] noun An object with many parts that work together to do a job

material [muh-TEER-ee-uhl] noun Something from which an object is made, or that is used for certain tasks

racket [RAK-it] noun A sport tool used to hit a ball

slate [sleyt] noun A tablet used for writing

travel [TRAV-uh l] verb To move from one place to another

A noun is a person, place, or thing.

A verb is an action word that tells you what someone or something does.

An adjective is a word that tells you what something is like.

Index

About the Author

Cynthia O'Brien has written many books for young readers. It is fun to help make a technology like a book! Books can be full of stories. They also teach you about the world around you, including other technologies.

To explore and learn more, enter the code at the Crabtree Plus website below.

www.crabtreeplus.com/fullsteamahead

Your code is:
fsa20

STEAM Notes for Educators

Full STEAM Ahead is a literacy series that helps readers build vocabulary, fluency, and comprehension while learning about big ideas in STEAM subjects. *Technology Then and Now* encourages readers to make connections in the text by comparing a technology that has changed over time. The STEAM activity below helps readers extend the ideas in the book to build their skills in technology, math, and science.

Making New Improvements

Children will be able to:
- Identify the specific types of changes made to improve different technologies.
- Create a plan to improve a technology using a specific type of change.

Materials
- Identifying Changes Chart
- Identifying Changes Chart Completed Example
- Challenge Sheet

Guiding Prompts
After reading *Technology Then and Now*, ask:
- Why do people change technologies over time? What are some ways they change?
- Can you think of a different example of a technology that has been improved over time? How was it improved?

Activity Prompts
Explain to children that we will explore some ways that technologies improve, then make a plan to improve our own technology!

Hand each child the Identifying Changes Chart. Have a full-size class version of the chart on chart paper, so the whole group can fill in the chart together. A chart with some completed examples has been provided for educator use. Each chart identifies methods by which technologies were improved.

When the chart is completed, discuss some ways that engineers have improved technologies over time. Then, hand children the Challenge Sheet. Outline the challenge for children.

In small groups of three to four, children will choose a technology that we use today and brainstorm how that technology might be improved, using one of the methods for improvement that were identified on the chart.

Have each group sketch their improved technology and write an explanation for how it was improved. Have children present their ideas.

Extensions
- Invite children to imagine one other method by which a technology could be improved. Apply that method to a current technology.

To view and download the worksheets, visit **www.crabtreebooks.com/resources/ printables** or **www.crabtreeplus.com/ fullsteamahead** and enter the code **fsa20**.